All Children Learn Differently
A Parent's Guide to Dyslexia

Mary Ball
Rosie Bissett
Anne Hughes
Wyn McCormack

ISBN 0-9532427-3-0

 **Vodafone
Ireland
Foundation**

The Dyslexia Association of Ireland acknowledges with gratitude, funding from
Vodafone Ireland Foundation which has made the production of this booklet possible.

Published by Dyslexia Association of Ireland
Printed by www.indianfield.ie
Designed by Siobhan O'Carroll

Contents

The Dyslexia Association of Ireland

The Dyslexia Association of Ireland (DAI) is a company, limited by guarantee which has charity status. It was founded in 1972 by parents and teachers who were concerned about the lack of awareness of dyslexia and the absence of provision for children with Dyslexia within the school system. The Dyslexia Association set about providing the information, psycho-educational assessment and specialist teaching which was needed. It is still doing so today, with more demand than ever for its services.

Membership

Any interested person may become a member of the Dyslexia Association. Only one membership is needed per family. The annual membership is €40 a year (from January 2008). Application forms are available on the website or at the back of this booklet.

Members receive a card each year which must be produced when enrolling a child at a DAI Workshop, Summer School or with a DAI listed tutor. Only members of the association may avail of these DAI services. We aim to send members about three newsletters a year, as well as mailing on upcoming DAI events. The DAI newsletter is crucial in keeping members up-to-date about dyslexia in Ireland, and DAI activities.

Membership fees also help to cover the costs of running the national association. By being a member of DAI you are part of a nation-wide organisation representing over 2,500 families and 35 branches. The money you give provides someone at the end of a phone to answer a query from a worried parent, advice for a teacher on availability of courses, a visit from a member of DAI to help a group set up a new branch.

Information

The first, and often the most crucial need of parents whose children are having learning difficulties is for information. The Dyslexia Association provides a public information service through a telephone helpline, printed information and a website www.dyslexia.ie. Members of the Association are kept up to date with developments through newsletters, public meetings and conferences. Courses for parents, talks to parent/teacher groups and in-service courses for teachers are also offered.

Psycho-educational Assessment

Many parents, who are unable to secure assessment for their children through the National Educational Psychological Service (NEPS) come to the Dyslexia Association. Parents can simply contact the association by phone or email and put the child's name on the waiting list. The DAI has been carrying out such assessments for over thirty years and provides a service for adults as well as children. Funding from the Further Education Section of the Department of Education and Science allows the Association to offer subsidised assessment to adults with limited means. The cost of psycho-educational assessment is €400 (2007). Waiting lists tend to be long, for both children and adults.

Branches – Almost Nationwide

The Dyslexia Association now has branches all around the country. Branches are run by voluntary committees of parents and teachers. They act as local parent support groups and lobbyists, raise awareness, provide information, fundraise and support the associated workshops. They also organise supplementary teaching by trained local teachers. Contact information for branches is available on the website www.dyslexia.ie

Group Tuition (DAI Workshops)

One of the earliest innovations of the Association, and one of the most successful, is the provision of group tuition for children between the ages of seven and seventeen, outside of school hours. Special classes are offered for students at Junior Certificate and Leaving Certificate level at some workshops and at 1 Suffolk Street, Dublin 2. Teaching is done by specifically trained teachers and the pupil teacher ratio is kept very low. Only children who have been diagnosed as having dyslexia may be enrolled. A full assessment report must be provided to the workshop so that a teaching programme appropriate to the child's needs may be implemented. Classes are usually held for two hours each week, between September and May, in a local school. Social and emotional development is fostered by interaction with other children with similar difficulties. Great emphasis is placed on the development of self-esteem and children are encouraged to believe in their own success. These classes, called workshops, are organised by voluntary branch committees and they are available in 35 locations around the country.

Fees are charged for attendance at workshops but every effort is made to accommodate students from financially disadvantaged families. Details of workshops can be found on the association's website, or by emailing info@dyslexia.ie

Individual Tuition

The association maintains a list of tutors who are willing to offer one-to-one tuition. These are trained teachers who have also taken a course in teaching children and adults with dyslexia. It must be stressed that the association's list is based solely on the educational qualifications of the teachers and is not a warranty in respect of any other matter whatever. The arrangement between student and teacher is a personal one and the Dyslexia Association does not accept liability in relation to this arrangement. In particular the Association is concerned that parents should be aware that the safety, well being and happiness of their child should be their first consideration in any arrangement they may enter into with a teacher. These tutors have not been subject to Garda vetting by DAI.

Parents and/or individuals with dyslexia may access names on this list by becoming members of the association. Individuals must have been assessed by a psychologist as having dyslexia and a copy of a written report must be available before tuition can commence. Tuition is usually carried out in the tutor's home. Tutors are available in most parts of the country.

In-service Courses for Teachers

In-service courses for qualified teachers are offered at weekends, evenings and during summer holidays. Full information is available on the website.

Parents' Courses and Talks

Short courses for parents on how to help and support their children are organised and speakers are available to give talks to parent/teacher groups, employers and others.

For further information contact the Dyslexia Association of Ireland:

By post: Suffolk Chambers,
1 Suffolk Street, Dublin 2

By phone: 01 6790276

By fax: 01 6790273

By email: info@dyslexia.ie

Online: www.dyslexia.ie

What is Dyslexia?

Dyslexia is a fundamental difficulty with language processing, particularly with written language. It is not caused by any physical or emotional difficulty. It is not a disease or defect; therefore it cannot be treated medically or cured. Dyslexic difficulties can be mild or severe and can occur in children at any level of intelligence. As dyslexia is genetic it does not go away and more than one child in a family may be affected. International research suggests that it affects between 6% and 8% of all children, though there are no definitive figures for Ireland. It is believed to be more common in boys than in girls. On the positive side children with dyslexia can and do learn to cope with it. Children with dyslexia learn differently but they do learn and many have very strong visual, creative, artistic and problem solving abilities.

Definitions

The word Dyslexia comes from the Greek dys meaning bad or difficult and lexis meaning word, vocabulary or language. There have been numerous definitions and descriptions of Dyslexia over the years. Most of them are long and technical but in simple terms Dyslexia can be described as a specific difficulty which makes it hard for some children to learn to read, write and spell correctly. Dyslexia can also affect the acquisition of maths.

The Task Force on Dyslexia, set up by the Minister for Education and Science, published its Report in July 2002. It defined dyslexia as follows:

Dyslexia is manifested in a continuum of specific learning difficulties related to the acquisition of basic skills in reading, spelling and/or writing, such difficulties being unexpected in relation to an individual's other abilities and educational experiences. Dyslexia can be described at the neurological, cognitive and behavioural levels. It is typically characterised by inefficient information processing, including difficulties in phonological processing, working memory, rapid naming and automaticity of basic skills. Difficulties in organisation, sequencing and motor skills may also be present.

(Task Force Report p.31)

Causes

There has been a great deal of research in recent years on the cause of dyslexia but it may be many years yet before a definitive answer is found. There are a number of theories. The most widely accepted one is that dyslexia is caused by a deficit in phonological processing. A phoneme is the smallest unit of sound in a word. In order to read one must be able to associate the letters on the page representing the phoneme with the corresponding speech sound. Evidence from brain imaging suggests that people with dyslexia do not activate the left hemisphere (the language side) in the brain as much when reading as non-dyslexic readers do, and that there is less engagement of the areas of the brain which match letters with sounds. This does not tell us why a phonological deficit occurs, but it is believed to be genetic, ie. that the child has inherited a gene which causes the brain to operate in this way.

Professor John Stein, Oxford, believes that auditory and visual difficulties are caused by abnormal magnocellular development. Malfunction in the development of sensory nerves happens at the foetal stage and is said to cause eye convergence difficulties and inhibit steady eye fixation.

Another view is that the role of the part of the brain which controls balance (the cerebellum) is crucial and that differences in this area make it difficult for children with dyslexia to acquire automaticity in tasks and may further inhibit the development of language dexterity and motor skills.

Other research suggests that there are different causes for different types of dyslexic difficulties and that the situation is often complicated by the co-existence of other specific learning difficulties such as attention deficit disorder or specific language impairment. It is known that genes on a number of chromosomes have been implicated in dyslexia so it is possible that combinations of genetic factors, coupled with other social and environmental factors account for the variations in the nature and extent of dyslexic type difficulties.

Dyslexia/Specific Learning Disability – What's the Difference?

Dyslexia is a specific learning disability, which means that the difficulty is specific to one area, in this case literacy. There are other specific learning difficulties such as Dyspraxia, ADD, ADHD, Specific Language Impairment, and Asperger's Syndrome. A child may have more than one of these conditions and it is important to determine which is the major difficulty.

The most prominent features of dyslexia are:
- Unexpected difficulty with literacy and number
- Difficulties in phonological awareness ie. ability to recognise the sound structures of a language
- Poor auditory working memory
- Delay in finding the right word (rapid naming)
- Delay in becoming automatic in a skill

Children with dyslexia may also experience difficulties with co-ordination and fine motor movement, ability to sequence and organise, delay in learning time, mixed laterality and problems with accurate direction.

How Would a Parent Recognise Dyslexia

The important thing for a child with Dyslexia is that, however it is defined, the condition is recognized and that appropriate intervention is put in place at the earliest possible time.

An unexpected problem in learning to read and/or spell should alert parents and teachers to the existence of a possible specific learning difficulty. There are many reasons why a child might experience difficulty or delay in reading and it is important to determine the exact cause. An eyesight or hearing problem, prolonged absence from school, frequent changes of school, emotional upset, specific language impairment or a general learning difficulty could all be causes or contributory factors to difficulties or delays in acquiring literacy and numeracy. Research indicates that if reading is not actively encouraged and supported in the home, and if teachers do not have a strong belief that the child can succeed, then reading and spelling levels can be adversely affected. A full psycho-educational assessment is necessary to provide a definite diagnosis of dyslexia and to rule out other causes of reading delay.

The Task Force on Dyslexia (2002) published a list of possible indicators of Dyslexia and these are re-printed below. When looking at the list of indicators please remember the following:
- No child will have all the indicators
- Many children will have several of the indicators
- Some indicators are more common than others
- The number of indicators observed in a child does not indicate whether the child's dyslexia is mild, moderate or severe

Indicators of Possible Learning Difficulty Arising from Dyslexia (Ages 3–5 Years)
- Is later than most children in learning to speak
- Has difficulty pronouncing some, especially multi-syllabic, words
- Has difficulty separating spoken words into sounds and blending spoken sounds to make words (ie. has difficulty with phonological awareness)
- Experiences auditory discrimination problem
- Is prone to spoonerisms (eg. Fips and chish for fish and chips.
- Has difficulty with rhyming
- Has difficulty maintaining rhythm
- Is unable to recall the right word
- Is slow to add new vocabulary
- Exhibits delays in acquiring emergent literacy skills (eg. understanding that written language progresses from left to right, discriminating between letters, words and sentences)
- Experiences problems learning the alphabet
- Has trouble learning numbers, days of the week, colours and shapes
- Has trouble learning to write and spell his/her own name

- Is unable to follow multi-step directions or routines
- Is developing fine motor skills more slowly than other children
- May have difficulty telling and/or retelling a story in correct sequence

Indicators of a Possible Learning Difficulty Arising from Dyslexia (Ages 5–7 Years)

- Is slow to learn the connection between letters and sounds (alphabetic principle)
- Has difficulty separating words into sounds, and blending sounds to form words (phonemic awareness)
- Has difficulty repeating multi-syllabic words (e.g. emeny for enemy, pasghetti for spaghetti)
- Has difficulty decoding single words (reading single words in isolation)
- Has poor word-attack skills, especially for new words.
- Confuses small or easy words: at/to; said/and; does/goes.
- May make constant reading and spelling errors including:
  Letter reversals (eg. d for b as in dog for bog)
  Letter inversions (eg. m for w)
  Letter transpositions (eg. felt and left)
  Word reversals (eg. tip for pit)
  Word substitutions (eg. house for home).
- Reads slowly with little expression or fluency (oral reading is slow and laborious)
- Has more difficulty with function words (eg. is, to, of) than with content words (eg. clouds, run, yellow)
- May be slow to learn new skills, relying heavily on memorising without understanding
- Reading comprehension is below expectation due to poor accuracy, fluency and speed

- Reading comprehension is better than single word reading
- Listening comprehension is better than reading comprehension
- Has trouble learning facts
- Has difficulty planning or organising
- Uses awkward pencil grip
- Has slow and poor quality handwriting
- Has trouble learning to tell the time on an analogue clock or watch
- Has poor fine motor co-ordination

Indicators of a Possible Learning Difficulty Arising from Dyslexia (Ages 7–12 Years)
- Has continued difficulty reading text aloud or silently
- Reading achievement is below expectation
- Still confuses letter sequences (eg. soiled for solid; left for felt)
- Is slow at discerning and learning prefixes, suffixes, root words and other morphemes as part of reading and spelling strategies
- Poor reading accuracy, fluency, or speed interferes with reading comprehension
- Spelling is inappropriate for age and general ability (eg. spelling the same word differently on the same page, use of bizarre spelling patterns, frequent letter omissions, additions and transposition)
- Poor spelling contributes to poor written expression (eg. may avoid use of unfamiliar words)
- Use avoidance tactics when asked to read orally or write
- Experiences language-related problems in Maths (eg. when reading word problems and directions, confuses numbers and symbols)

- Is unable to learn multiplication tables by rote
- Still confuses some directional words
  (eg. left and right)
- Has slow or poor recall of facts
- Lacks understanding of other people's body language
  and facial expressions
- Has trouble with non-literal or figurative language
  (eg. idioms, proverbs)
- Forgets to bring in or hand in homework
- Has difficulty remembering what day or month it is
- Has difficulty remembering his/her own telephone
  number or birthday
- Has poor planning and organisational skills
- Has poor time management
- Lacks self-confidence and has a poor self-image

Indicators of a Possible Learning Difficulty Arising from Dyslexia (Ages 12 Years+)

- Is still reading slowly and without fluency,
  with many inaccuracies
- Misreads words (eg. hysterical for historical)
  or information
- Has difficulty modifying reading rate
- Has an inadequate store of knowledge due to lack
  of reading experience
- Continues to experience serious spelling difficulties
- Has slow, dysfluent and/or illegible handwriting
- Has better oral skills than written skills
- Has difficulty planning, sequencing and organising
  written text
- Has difficulty with written syntax or punctuation
- Has difficulty skimming, scanning and/or proof
  reading written text
- Has trouble summarising or outlining.

- Has problems in taking notes and copying from the board
- Procrastinates and/or avoids reading and writing tasks
- Does not complete assignments or class work or does not hand them in
- Is slow in answering questions, especially open-ended ones
- Has poor memorisation skills
- Still mispronounces or misuses some words.
- Has problems recalling the names of some words or objects
- Has poor planning and organisation skills
- Has poor time management skills
- Has more difficulty in language-based subjects (eg. English, Irish, History) than in non-language based subjects (eg. Mathematics, Technical Graphics)
- Lacks self-confidence and has poor self-image

(Task Force Report pp. 66-75)

Psycho-educational Assessment

Parents who suspect that a child may have dyslexia should take action. Dyslexia does not go away if ignored. If left untreated, Dyslexia can stop a child from mastering the basics of reading, writing and arithmetic, damage self-esteem and have negative long-term effects. There is ample evidence from research to demonstrate the benefits of early intervention, but it is not always clear how best to help the child. The purpose of a psycho-educational assessment is to determine if a learning difficulty exists, and if it does, to explore the nature and extent of the problem and to advise on the best possible learning support.

School Based Assessment

Parents who are worried about a child's progress in school should first approach the class teacher, who may give some screening tests. If a problem persists the class teacher will usually refer to the special needs or learning support teacher to arrange additional tuition. If substantial progress is not made within a couple of terms and teachers and parents are still worried, the school principal may refer the child's name to the National Educational Psychological Service (NEPS). Psycho-educational assessments carried out by NEPS are done in the school and free of charge. However, it can be difficult to secure an assessment in this way as availability is limited and schools have to prioritise the students most in need. Preference may be given to younger children and it can be particularly difficult to arrange a review of progress or re-assessment of an older child at primary school.

Private Assessment

Because of the long waiting time, many parents opt for private assessment, either with the Dyslexia Association of Ireland or with a psychologist in private practice. A list of the latter is available on the website of the Psychological Society of Ireland www.psihq.ie Private assessment costs from €400 to €600. Tax relief is available on the fees paid for private assessments. This is claimed by using the MED 1 form when completing year end tax returns.

A full psycho-educational assessment can take between two and three hours. A detailed family history, a school report and a short interview with parents are usually required before assessment. The assessment itself includes intelligence testing, as well as tests to assess the level of word reading, reading comprehension, spelling and mathematics. Feedback may be given to parents immediately following assessment, with a more detailed written report supplied later. Ideally this report will contain advice on the teaching approach most likely to benefit the child, taking his/her learning strengths and weaknesses into account.

Preparing a Child for Assessment

It is worth remembering that IQ (intelligence quotient) tests measure certain abilities, but they do not cover the full range of human abilities. IQ tests are believed to be an indicator of how an individual is likely to achieve within a formal learning environment, but not of how that person will fare in working and social life. Many people who have been very successful in life did not perform well while at school.

Having an assessment with a psychologist should be a pleasant event in a child's life. Many children are happy to discover the reason why they experience difficulty with learning and relieved to discover that it is not due to their own lack of effort. Unfortunately, sometimes it is upsetting for both child and parent. A little preparatory work should prevent that happening. Some common sense points to bear in mind are listed below.

- Choose your psychologist carefully to ensure that s/he is familiar with Specific Learning Difficulty/Dyslexia.
- Find out as much as you can about the assessment procedure in advance.
- The more informed you are the more relaxed you will be and this will be beneficial to the child.
- Be as honest and frank as you can.
- Tell the child why you are visiting a psychologist, ie. because the child is having some difficulty – reading, writing or spelling.
- Present it in the most positive way you can – as something you have arranged specially so that you can help.
- Explain what the psychologist will do, ie. she will talk to the child about school, ask questions, give certain tasks, some oral, some written, some practical and some visual.
- Explain that this is not an exam. The child cannot fail. The psychologist will only be interested in finding out how the child thinks and learns.
- Tell your child where you are going, at what time and how long it will take.
- Try to ensure that the child is well rested.
- Bring a nutritious snack if necessary.
- If possible, build in a little treat afterwards.

- After the assessment the psychologist will probably give you some brief feedback. Using your own good judgment, tell the child as simply as possible what the psychologist said, always stressing the most positive things. If you are upset or anxious about what you have been told, wait until you are feeling more positive before saying very much to your child

Understanding the Assessment Report
The psycho-educational assessment usually consists of a test of general intellectual functioning as well as tests of levels of literacy and phonological awareness Further tests may be given if the psychologist feels she needs more information on any area eg. movement, social and emotional factors, attention. There are many test materials on the market Psychologists use those which they find will give them most reliable information, i.e. those which have been tried and standardized on large populations of children and which have a valid theoretical basis. The following are among the most frequently used in this country, but are not the only ones.

Tests Materials Which May be Used

Intelligence scales
- Wechsler Intelligence Scale for Children, 4th Edition (WISC-IV)
- British Ability Scales
- Stanford Binet Intelligence Scales

Tests of Reading and Writing
- Wechsler Individual Attainment Tests, 2nd Edition (WIAT-11)
- Neale Analysis of Reading Ability NARA
- Woodcock-Johnson tests of achievement
- Wide Range Achievement Tests 4

Test of Phonological Awareness
- Phonological Assessment Battery PhAB

Dyslexia Screening Tests
- Dyslexia Early Screening Test
- Dyslexia Screening Test
- Bangor Dyslexia Test

Intelligence tests measure a wide range of abilities, some verbal, some visual spatial. The WISC-IV is the intelligence test most widely used in this country. The results you will find printed in your report will include a Full Scale IQ, which is obtained from the scores of the ten individual tests given. Results will also describe your child's present functioning over four intellectual domains and the results will be quoted as 'Composite scores'. The domains or aspects of ability are Verbal Comprehension (a verbal cluster of abilities), Perceptual Reasoning (non-verbal abilities), Working Memory (auditory memory and sequencing) and Processing Speed (involving hand-eye co-ordination, visual memory and discrimination).

To the psychologist and to the parent it is important to note the cluster scores as well as the Full Scale score. They give a great deal of information eg. on a 'dyslexic' profile Working Memory and Processing Speed may be considerably weaker than Verbal Comprehension and Perceptual Reasoning.

Each child's profile will be different, presenting a picture of individual strengths and weaknesses. Whichever test of intelligence is used, the value of the information is in helping to identify a source of processing difficulty which may explain the literacy delay. It also helps parent and teacher to understand how the child learns. By looking at her strengths and weaknesses one can construct a personal approach that will help the child to use her strengths to develop strategies to support and compensate for learning difficulties.

The Numbers Game

Psycho-educational assessment reports often have a lot of numbers and percentages and, not surprisingly, many parents find this confusing, particularly as some scales are from 1–130, some from 1–19 and some figures are in percentiles.

IQ scores are recorded on a scale of 1–130+, with 100 as the mid-point.

Standard Scores

Standard scores are a means of being able to compare results of children of the same age and to say how far the score is above or below the 'average'. They are usually calculated on a scale of 1–130+ with a score of 100 being the mid-point of 'average'. Standard scores are used for attainment tests as well as IQ tests.

There are two types of standard scores on the WISC IV, Scaled scores and Composite scores

Scaled Scores: recorded on a scale 1–19. Here 10 is the mid-point and represents the 'average' performance of a given age group.

Composite Scores: these are on a scale 1–130+. These describe the combining of individual subtest results into a category of abilities or attainments eg. Verbal Comprehension Composite score is made up of results from subtests Vocabulary, Similarities and Comprehension; Reading Composite score is made up of results from the Word Reading, Pseudoword Reading and Reading Comprehension subtests.

Composite scores (ie. Verbal Comprehension Index, Perceptual Reasoning Index, Working Memory Index, Processing Speed Index and Full Scale IQ). can be given qualitative descriptions and percentile ranking as follows:

Composite/IQ	Classification	Percentile Rank Equivalent
130 and above	Very Superior	98–100
120–129	Superior	91–97
110–119	High Average	75–90
90–109	Average	25–74
80–89	Low Average	09–24
70–79	Borderline	02–08
69 and below	Extremely Low	01–

Percentile Rank: on a scale 1–100.
A percentile is the point at which the child would come in a group of 100 children of the child's age, eg. a percentile of 75 means that this child has achieved as well as 75% of children and only 25% of children of the same age would be expected to achieve a higher score.

Confidence Interval: this is like a margin of error. On another day the child may achieve a slightly higher or a slightly lower score within the figures given eg. if a child's IQ score is 100 the confidence interval may be 95-105.

Tests of Attainment
Reading tests will include tests of ability to recognise individual words, to read and understand passages and to read unfamiliar words.

Tests of writing will typically include a spelling test, free writing and writing speed, depending on what stage the child is at.

When the Wechsler Individual Attainment Test (WIAT-11) is given during a psycho-educational assessment the following areas may be tested:

- **Reading** – word reading, reading comprehension, pseudoword decoding
- **Mathematics** – numerical operations and mathematics reasoning
- **Written Language** – spelling and written expression
- **Oral Language** – listening comprehension and oral expression

Often time does not permit the psychologist to administer all, except in exceptional circumstances where she may need to get as much information as possible. The WISC and WIAT are lengthy tests to administer.

Test scores are usually standard scores; percentiles and age equivalents are usually given also. The standard scores from the WISC and the WIAT can be compared ie. at each age level and each IQ level there is an expected score. When a child has a score 'significantly' below this expected score the psychologist must draw conclusions about the possible reason for the discrepancy, from all the information she has received and from evidence from all her test results. A wide discrepancy may confirm the presence of dyslexia.

After the Assessment

Getting a psycho-educational assessment can be a time consuming and expensive process so parents will want to know – what next? It is very important to follow up on the recommendations made in the assessment report, but first both parents and child must come to terms with what they have learned.

Telling Your Child About Dyslexia

If a diagnosis of dyslexia has been made and your child needs to have extra tuition, attend a workshop, a Special Reading School or Special Needs teacher at school, this will need to be explained to the child very carefully. Again, the more information a parent has the easier this will be. There is a lot of information now available on Dyslexia. When explaining dyslexia to your child, however, you have to translate this into plain language. You also want the child to know that dyslexia is nothing to be ashamed of, that help is available and that there is no reason why the child should not achieve his or her potential.

- If your child is diagnosed as having Dyslexia then tell your child this. there is no reason to hide it.
- Explain that dyslexia is a very common condition and several other people in the school and maybe one or two in his/her class, or in the family also have it

- You can tell the child that dyslexia is just a big word to explain why some children find it hard to learn to read, write and spell. Everyone is different. We all have different strengths and weaknesses. Identify something the child does very well, whether it is sport, music, art or hand work. It could be that the child is good with animals, generous, popular, funny, loving – whatever. Find some real strength which the child has. This is most important. Then say that the child does not find reading and spelling as easy as these other things, but that is how life is.
- Explain that this is not the fault of the child, the parent or the school. It is something that happens – like having fair hair or freckles or blue eyes.
- Let the child know that this explains why s/he is having difficulty at school.
- Tell him/her that this means s/he will have to work very hard, maybe harder than others in the class to succeed but that it can be done, with proper help and support.
- Be prepared to discuss the issue with your child more than once. Do not assume that s/he will take it all in the first time. You may need to return to the subject over the coming years.
- If you have been angry with or critical of your child in the past because of home-work/school difficulties then this is the time to apologise. Don't be afraid to say that you were wrong. Children can be very forgiving.
- If extra help is needed, either with a Special Needs Teacher or outside of school, present this in the most positive light – as help rather than punishment.
- If extra help clashes with an activity which brings the child success, think very carefully before disturbing this arrangement.

- Make sure the child knows that while school work is very important it is just one aspect of life.
- Ensure that the child knows that your love is not dependent on good results in school work, that you value him or her for his/her own sake.
- If you are telling relatives or friends about the diagnosis of dyslexia in the child's hearing, be very careful to be as positive as possible and not to tell them a different story than you told the child. Children very quickly pick up on discrepancies between what they've been told and what you really think.

Of course, all of this is easier said than done. It is hard, initially, to avoid a sense of panic when you get a diagnosis of dyslexia. You may think – 'why my child', 'it's not fair'. This is perfectly natural, but once the first shock has passed, energy is best directed into seeking practical ways to help your child. When you get to this stage you may find the support available from other parents in your area invaluable. There are branches of the Dyslexia Association all around the country and a volunteer parent is often on hand to take calls. A contact list is available on the website www.dyslexia.ie The association runs short courses for parents and provides a great deal of information and support to members. The Dyslexia Association has been providing a telephone helpline for members of the public for over 30 years and the number is 01 6790276.

What does the future hold?

'Where will my child end up?' This is a very common question from parents of children with Dyslexia. It's not an easy one to answer, as indeed it is hard to predict what life path any child will choose. We do know that the extent to which Dyslexia affects a child's future depends on the severity of the disability, the age at which it is identified and the amount of support offered.

Late identification or an unsympathetic approach can cause extra problems. Such children may begin withdrawing emotionally if they are failing consistently at school. Others may withdraw physically and truancy could be a problem. Others may be very reluctant to go to school. Some may become troublesome and aggressive in class and set out to wreck a system that seems to them unfair. Others may deny that there is a problem at all and may need counselling and support before they let someone help them.

The positive news is that there has never been more awareness of Dyslexia and that better strategies for dealing with it are being researched all the time. There are many ways in which parents and teachers can help and some of these are detailed elsewhere in this booklet. There is also ample evidence that people with dyslexia have been successful in all walks of life as the following list shows:

Actors & Entertainers
John Lennon
Anthony Hopkins
Robbie Williams
Eddie Izzard
Susan Hampshire
Marlon Brando
Billy Bob Thornton
Kirsty Alsopp
Damon Albarn
Orlando Bloom
Cher
Dustin Hoffman
Jay Leno
River Phoenix
Ruby Wax

Artists & Designers
Pauline Bewick
Leonardo daVinci
Walt Disney
Charles Rennie Mackintosh
Pablo Picasso
Auguste Rodin
Anthony Gormley
Steven Spielberg
Tommy Hilfiger

Businessmen & Entrepreneurs
Richard Branson
Steve Jobs
Ingvar Kamprad (Ikea)
Lord McAlpine
Bill Gates

Inventors & Scientists
Thomas Alva Edison
Albert Einstein
Michael Faraday
Alexander Graham Bell
Jack Horner

Athletes & Sportspersons
Muhammad Ali
Magic Johnson
Sir Steve Redgrave
Sir Jackie Stewart
Sandy Lyle

Writers & Poets
Agatha Christie
Roald Dahl
John Irving
Don Mullan
Lynda la Plante
William Butler Yeats
Murray Lachlan Young
Benjamin Zephaniah
Lord Richard Rogers

Celebrity Chefs
Jamie Oliver
Rick Stein
Marco Pierre White

Other Specific Learning Difficulties

The term dyslexia is often written as being synonymous with the terms specific learning difficulties/specific learning disability. This can be very confusing. The term specific learning disability includes dyslexia as one of a number of specific, as distinct from general learning disabilities. Dyslexia is specific to certain aspects of learning. Very often the person with reading difficulty scores in the average or above average ranges on an intelligence test. Thus the difficulty is not the result of overall or general learning disability. Psychologists in reports often describe a child as having a specific learning difficulty of a dyslexic nature.

Since the mid-1990s the term specific learning disability has been used to include dyslexia, dyspraxia, specific language impairment (SLI), attention deficit disorder (ADD)/attention deficit hyperactivity disorder (ADHD) and autistic spectrum disorder. Of these disabilities dyslexia is probably the most recognised. Unfortunately children with dyslexia may also have one or more of the other specific learning disabilities. Research indicates that between 40 and 45 per cent of children with dyspraxia also have dyslexia, and that around 50 per cent of children with dyslexia also have ADHD. There is also evidence of an overlap between dyslexia and language impairment. The following brief explanations are given below, but more detailed information about these specific learning difficulties with regard to assessment and support can best be obtained from the relevant organisations:

The Dyspraxia Association, 69A Main Street, Leixlip,
Co. Kildare. Ph. 01 2957125 www.dyspraxiaireland.com

HADD (for Attention Deficit Disorders),
Carmichael House, North Brunswick Street, Dublin 7.
Ph. 01 8748349 (Wednesday/Friday mornings)

Aspire (for Autistic Spectrum Disorders),
Carmichael House, North Brunswick Street, Dublin 7.
Ph. 01 8780027 www.aspire-irl.com

Dyspraxia

The term dyspraxia comes from the root dus/dys
meaning bad or difficult and praxis meaning movement
or action. Developmental dyspraxia is the term used
to describe a condition whereby the child has more
than usual difficulty with co-ordination, with organising
movement and also often has significant visual
perceptual difficulties. In some literature it can be
referred to as developmental co-ordination disorder
(DCD). The difficulties the child experiences are not
caused by other recognised conditions, such as
cerebral palsy, multiple sclerosis or hemiplegia. In early
childhood the features most noticeable include:

- Difficulty articulating words
- Difficulty dressing oneself
- Limited concentration
- Difficulty following instructions
- Sensitivity to noise and changing light
- Difficulty with spatial perception resulting in bumping
  into things, being clumsy and falling over easily

Attention Deficit/Hyperactivity Disorders (ADD and ADHD)

ADD/ADHD describes a condition where the child has more than usual difficulty maintaining attention for any length of time, is highly distractible, disorganised, forgetful and appears not to listen to instructions. These children may also be over-active, fidgety, want everything instantly and be impulsive. Many people associate ADHD with hyperactivity, that is, they focus on the most obvious indicator, the child's difficulty with staying still and the need to be constantly on the go. However, since 1994, a significant distinction has been made between ADD (Attention Deficit Disorder) and ADHD (Attention Deficit Hyperactivity Disorder). In the first case the child does not exhibit the hyper activity of the second case. In both cases the core difficulty is with ability to control attention.

The following is a checklist of some of the items which describe a child with ADD.

- Difficulty concentrating, except on activities of personal interest
- Highly distractible
- Inconsistent – good days/bad days
- Disorganised
- Difficulty following through instructions
- Poor perseverance except on tasks enjoyed
- Pays little attention to detail
- Forgetful and dreamy

In addition to the above, the child with ADHD manifests behaviours such as the following:

- Unable to stay seated for any length
- Fidgety, restless and constantly touching things
- Asks questions impulsively, interrupts, makes inappropriate comments and/or makes vocal noises
- Needs to be moving most of the time
- Has difficulty in controlling impulses
- Can be impatient and demanding of instant response
- Cannot queue in lines
- Acts first, thinks later

As with dyslexia and dyspraxia, any two children with ADHD/ADD may have quite different profiles because their combination of difficulties places them at different points along a continuum of difficulties. It is important to note that their poor reading and writing development may not be rooted in dyslexia but result from their difficulty focusing attention long enough to get a grasp of basic instructions.

Asperger's Syndrome

The term Asperger's Syndrome came into use as recently as 1983, in a paper published by Burgoine and Wing which describes the features that are considered to characterise the disability. In the 1940s a Viennese paediatrician, Hans Asperger, had already identified these, hence the name. Asperger's Syndrome is usually classified under the Autistic Spectrum Disorders. In the United States and in some English-speaking countries it is referred to as 'high-functioning autism'. Asperger's Syndrome/Disorder describes the social components of autism but without the significant impairments of learning and language that characterise autism.

The following are the core features of Asperger's Syndrome:

- Lack of empathy
- Poor ability to form friendships
- One-sided conversations
- Intense absorption in a special interest
- Poor verbal communication
- Odd postures and clumsy movements

It should be remembered that the presence of any one or any cluster of these features do not in themselves indicate Asperger's Disorder, for example, poor communication skills, and consequently poor ability to hold a two-sided conversation, may be caused by a language disorder. The only way to get a true diagnosis is to have an appropriate assessment which is wide-ranging and thorough. Aspire, the Asperger's Syndrome organisation will provide advice on where to look for this.

Specific Language Impairment (SLI)

Although specific language impairment (SLI) is not strictly classified as a specific learning difficulty, many children with dyslexia have experienced specific language delay. They may have required speech therapy, usually at the pre-school and kindergarten stage. Specific language delay can occur in either or both of the areas of expression and reception. The difficulties may be at the level of phonology (discrimination of different sounds, recognition of similar sounds), semantics (understanding meaning), syntax (grammatical structure of sentence), pragmatics (using language suited to what they want to communicate) and fluency. Recent studies in Britain by Professor Margaret Snowling have identified reading comprehension difficulties in significant numbers of children. The studies also suggest that children with poor oral language skills are at high risk of literacy failure. Dyslexia and language difficulties often co-exist. This is why a psychologist assessing for dyslexia may sometimes recommend a further assessment by a speech and language therapist.

Provision in the Irish School System

In recent years legislation has been enacted in relation to the provision of education for children in Ireland. Some of these are more relevant to children with Dyslexia than others. The following is a summary. More information is available in Dyslexia – An Irish Perspective, Chapter 4. and Lost for Words.

The Education Act 1998

This Act states that the school shall provide education for students which is appropriate to their abilities and needs. It also states that schools must have and publish a policy on its admission procedures, including those for students with disabilities. This is very important in view of the difficulties which many parents have reported in gaining a place for a student in a school of their choice.

The Education (Welfare) Act 2000

This Act safeguards every child's entitlement to an appropriate minimum education. It established the National Educational Welfare Board, which plays a key role in relation to issues like absenteeism.

The Education of Persons with Special Educational Needs Act 2004

This Act is very relevant. Its definition of special educational needs (SEN) includes any condition 'which results in a person learning differently from a person without that condition'. This gives students with Dyslexia certain rights and entitlements, including the right to have an assessment carried out at the request of the school principal, and to the subsequent preparation of a plan for the 'appropriate education of the student'.

The Act also set up the National Council for Special Education (NCSE) which is the body now responsible for overseeing services for students with special educational needs in schools. The Council employs Special Educational Needs Organisers (SENOs) who decide on applications from schools for extra resources for students with SEN.

The Act contains an appeals procedure for parents if they believe the special educational needs of their child are not being addressed.

Psycho-Educational Assessment

In theory, a student attending primary or second level school is entitled to have a psycho-educational assessment carried out if the school principal has reached the opinion that a student is not benefiting from the education programme provided and may have special educational needs.

This assessment should be carried out free of charge by a psychologist from the National Educational Psychological Service. Unfortunately, due to staff shortages and pressures of other work it is not always possible to secure an assessment by this means. However, it is always worthwhile requesting such an assessment. The NEPS website is found on the Department of Education and Science website www.education.ie.

If the assessment establishes that the student has special educational needs, the principal should arrange for an individual education plan to be drawn up. If the student meets the criteria for learning support an individual profile and learning programme (IPLP) should be drawn up. These should outline the learning programme to be followed by the child and they set out targets which should be reviewed regularly. Parents are entitled to be consulted and involved in this procedure, together with the class teacher, special needs teachers and professionals involved in the assessment procedure.

Additional Teaching Support
The Department of Education and Science (DES) provides additional teaching support for students with dyslexia in three different ways.

- Extra teaching support through the provision of learning support
- Special classes attached to a mainstream school
- Special schools for children with specific learning difficulties

This support is targeted at those students in greatest need as defined by the Department of Education and Science criteria. As a result not all students with dyslexia qualify for such support. Recent changes in the provision of learning support mean that this is now provided by special needs teachers. Children do not need to have had a psycho-educational assessment to get access to extra support. If the class teacher and parents feel that a child is not progressing satisfactorily in the mainstream class, the student may receive support from the special needs teacher. This is dependent on the availability of the SEN teacher.

Schools are allocated such teaching posts on the basis of the number of students enrolled, not on an assessment of individual need. It is possible therefore for a child with a significant delay in reading to receive learning support in one school, while a child with the same delay in another school may not.

Children with dyslexia are regarded as having a 'high incidence' disability and it is felt that they are best helped by support from the SEN teacher. In effect this usually means tuition in small groups of children with different educational needs.

At present, second level students performing at the 2nd percentile or less in standardised literacy tests may be eligible for one-to-one resource teaching. An application has to be made by the school to the local SENO requesting additional resources for the student.

Note: The fact that a child does not need to have a diagnosis of dyslexia in order to get support from the SEN teacher is not always a good thing. While it is important that a child with reading delay should receive early and appropriate support, it is very important that the precise reason for the reading delay should be investigated. This is necessary in order to provide the most effective intervention. A child with dyslexia requires different teaching strategies to those required by children with other learning difficulties.

It is also important to note that a psycho-educational assessment is still necessary when applying for a place at a reading school; or for exemption from the study of Irish; for reasonable accommodation in state exams at Leaving Certificate; when applying for grants for assistive technology and support services at third level.

Special Classes attached to Mainstream Schools
Children who have been assessed by a psychologist as having average ability or above and whose literacy attainments are "at a very low level compared to the vast majority of students in a similar age cohort" may be eligible to enrol in special reading classes. Such children will usually have literacy attainments at the 5th percentile or lower). These classes (called reading units) are attached to mainstream schools and students participate in some joint activities with the other students. The pupil teacher ratio is 9:1. Enrolment is usually for two years only, at the end of which the child returns to the school he or she previously attended. There are nineteen such units throughout the country. The Department of Education and Science website gives details of locations.

Special Schools for Children with Specific Learning Difficulties

The Department of Education and Science has established four primary schools for students with specific learning difficulties including those arising from dyslexia. These schools are as follows:

St. Killian's   Bishopstown, Cork.
St. Oliver Plunkett's   Monkstown, Co. Dublin.
Catherine McAuley's   59 Lr. Baggot St, Dublin 2.
St. Rose's   Balrothery, Tallaght, Dublin 24.

The criteria for access to these schools is similar to those for access to special classes, and attendance is usually for two years only, though in exceptional circumstances a third year may be allowed.

Exemption from studying Irish

Students are not allowed exemption from the study of Irish just because they have dyslexia, or because they find the language difficult. Irish is a compulsory subject for students in primary and post-primary schools. However students with dyslexia may be granted an exemption. The exemption is given to students who have average or above average intellectual ability but whose English reading and spelling levels place them at the 10th percentile of their age group, or less. Circular M10/94 sets out the details regarding the exemption from Irish.

The procedure for gaining an exemption involves the parent submitting a written application on behalf of the child to the school principal along with a copy of a report from a psycho-educational assessment that is less than two years old and which recommends that the student should be exempt because the criteria are met.

If the school authorities grant an exemption, a certificate is issued and the Department of Education and Science is informed. The exemption granted at primary level will be recognised at second level and for entry to the National University of Ireland (NUI) colleges. The exemption should be taken into account at entrance assessment when students are transferring to second-level if Irish is included as part of the assessment.

There are some careers where a certain standard of Irish is required. A 'C' in higher level Irish in the Leaving Certificate is necessary for primary teaching. Irish is also required for certain teaching courses at second level and it is always wise to check the course requirements carefully before applying if an Irish exemption is in place. It is no longer mandatory for entrance to the Garda Siochana but it should be noted that English and one other language are required. Irish may be the second language and if so a 'C' 3 grade at foundation level in Irish is sufficient. It should also be noted that all trainee Gardai are required to take a course in basic Irish.

Sometimes a teacher at primary level, recognising the child's difficulties, allows the child to do extra English work during the allocated time for Irish. However the official exemption is not issued. If the student is not studying Irish at primary level, it is very important for a parent to ask the school for the certificate of exemption. Otherwise the child will be required to study Irish when attending second-level.

Exemption from the NUI Third Language Requirement

The National University of Ireland (NUI) comprises the colleges of UCC, UCD, UCG and Maynooth and some other smaller colleges. The entry requirements for NUI colleges specify that a student must pass six subjects in the Leaving Certificate, two at higher level, and that the student must include English, Irish and a third language.

NUI recognises the exemption from Irish granted at primary or post primary and also allows a student with such an exemption to be exempt from the third language requirement for entry to NUI. This means that students do not have to take Irish and a third language as subjects in the Leaving Certificate. It is important to apply to NUI, preferably during fifth year, for recognition of the Irish exemption and to apply for the third language exemption.

If students are not exempt from Irish, they may still qualify for an exemption from the third language requirement. NUI considers applications for such an exemption from students who are certified by a qualified professional as having a serious dyslexic condition. The application should be made prior to entry to senior cycle at second level, before subject choice for the Leaving Certificate has been made. Forms are available in the Entry Requirements section on the NUI website www.nui.ie.

Most other third level colleges, eg. Trinity, DCU, DIT and the ITs require English plus one other language. Students who have a certified exemption from Irish at primary/post-primary level will generally be given an exemption from the second language requirement. Separate application will need to be made to each college to which the student is applying.

Distinction between entry requirements and course requirements

While a student may have an exemption from a second or third language requirement for entry to a college, certain courses require that a language be studied as part of the course. For example a business or engineering course may include modules on German, French or Spanish. It is essential to check on the precise language requirements for each course before applying. This can be done by reading the college brochures. If in any doubt, consult the relevant college department. It is important to check this out for all colleges not just the NUI colleges.

Grants for the purchase of equipment

Students who have been diagnosed by a psychologist as having Dyslexia may be entitled to assistive technology. The school the student attends may apply to buy a computer and/or other software deemed necessary by the assessing psychologist. The criterion is that the student should have a very significant literacy difficulty (attaining at the 2nd percentile or less). Examples of such equipment include computers, tape-recorders and word processors. The application is made by the school to the SENO and must be accompanied by a comprehensive professional assessment.

If parents buy a computer and/or software for a child with dyslexia for home/personal use, the VAT can be claimed back, using Form VAT 61A, from the VAT Repayments Section, Revenue Commissioners, The Plantation, Monaghan. Tel. 047 81425. Forms can be downloaded from the website www.revenue.ie

Second Level Schooling

Choosing a second level school

Finding a second-level school to meet the needs of a student with dyslexia can be very difficult. Unfortunately this is getting more difficult as time goes on because not all schools welcome children with special educational needs. This has led some parents to secure a place for their child first and then discuss his/her needs for support afterwards. Not all parents are happy with this approach and feel that if a school does not want their child then its best not to enroll him/her.

There is no such thing as the perfect school for students with dyslexia, but making the best choice possible requires some research and forward planning.

(More detailed information can be found in Dyslexia – an Irish Perspective, Chapter 8).

Points to consider

Location – can the student get there relatively easily? Is this school attended by other children in the area? This can be important for making friends locally and being part of the community.

Philosophy – is the school open to accepting students who learn differently. For example, students with dyslexia tend to be forgetful and disorganized, how will the school cope with this? It is important to visit the school and discuss these issues with the principal before enrolment.

Size of school – smaller schools and smaller class size may suit a student with dyslexia as teachers may know him/her personally? Larger schools tend to have a wider range of subjects to choose from and may have more sporting and extra curricular activities. These can be very important in giving a student success in areas other than in academic learning.

Class Placement – are classes of mixed ability or streamed. This is a contentious subject and much research has been done in the area. Mixed ability seems to have the greatest advantages for students with dyslexia. In this situation the students are selected at random and will have a mix of abilities and disabilities. The student who is capable of understanding and dealing with complex material, but whose reading and spelling is delayed, will be challenged and stretched in a way which would not happen in a lower ability situation.

Streamed classes place students according to their performance on an initial assessment. There will be different ability levels, depending on the number of students. Parents will remember the concept of the A Class, all the way down to the D or E class. The de-motivation of being placed in the D or E class is very significant, particularly for a student whose ability exceeds their literacy attainment.

Some schools use a system called 'setting' which can be very helpful for students with dyslexia. Students may be placed in a higher class for maths and a weaker class for English or Irish. This allows them to be part of the mainstream class but take subjects at Higher or Ordinary level.

Subject Choice

At primary level children must study what is laid down for them. Much of the time will be taken up with reading, writing, spelling and arithmetic. At second level, particularly after Junior Certificate some choices are possible. These choices may have a major impact on third level options so they need to be considered carefully. Entry to the colleges in the Central Applications Office (CAO) system is based on the points system. Students need to be able to present their six best subjects in the Leaving Certificate if they are to achieve their best possible points score. Choosing subjects carefully to play to the strengths of the individual student is vital. Choices will of course be limited by school timetables, but at Leaving Certificate level it is worth looking at the option of taking an extra subject outside of school if an advantage can be gained.
(see Dyslexia – an Irish Perspective, and Lost for Words for more information.)

Irish, English and Mathematics are compulsory subjects at second level, unless a student has been given an official exemption from the study of Irish. Most schools also require students to take a modern foreign language as well. This can be difficult for students with dyslexia as languages tend to be their weakest subjects. However, students who have good aural and oral ability may do well in languages, particularly in the oral and aural parts of examinations. It is a widely-held belief that a student needs a foreign language for entry to third level. However, it is only in the National University of Ireland (NUI) colleges that this is an entry requirement and the student with dyslexia may apply for an exemption. Other third-level colleges do not require that students have a foreign language for entry to the college.

Subjects that require answers containing factual information may be easier than subjects in which answers are in essay-type format, where the student has to analyse and sequence information to structure the answer. Therefore, it may be easier to achieve good marks in Science rather than in English or History.

Some subjects such as Technical Graphics, Maths and Accounting rely on the student learning skills by doing several examples of the same task with different information. There is less of a reliance on memorising of facts. For the student with short-term memory difficulties, this may help.

Some students with dyslexia have excellent spatial/visual relations and will do well in subjects such as Art, Construction Studies and Technical Graphics.

Continuous assessment may help the student with short-term memory difficulties. Some subjects such as Art, Home Economics, Engineering, Construction Studies and Religion have a project or journal to be filled in prior to the terminal exam and marks are awarded for such work.

Reasonable Accommodation in State Examinations

Reasonable accommodation is the phrase used to describe the various types of support provided for students in the state examinations. These arrangements are only made when a student has good knowledge of the course content but lacks the reading, spelling or grammatical skills to demonstrate that knowledge.

The types of accommodation include:

- The provision of a person to read examination questions. Questions can be read as often as required, but no explanations or definitions can be given. An explanatory note is attached to the statement of results and the certificate of students who avail of a reader saying 'all parts of the examination in this subject were examined except the reading element'.
- Use of tape recorder or computer to record answers. The annotation for this accommodation reads 'all parts of the examination in this subject were assessed except spelling and some grammatical elements'.
- A waiver from the spelling and grammatical components in language subjects. This means that marks are not deducted for mistakes in spelling or in grammar. This applies only to language exams. Marks are not deducted for spelling or grammatical errors in other subjects. A similar annotation to that for use of tape recorder or computer is attached to the statement of marks and final certificate.

Students, who are given the accommodation of taping, use of reader or use of word processor, take the examinations in a centre by themselves with a supervisor. Students, who have been granted the accommodation of a waiver from spelling and grammar, take the examination in the main examination centre.

When using a tape recorder, the student needs practice in answering questions in this fashion and needs to be thoroughly familiar with using the equipment. Likewise, students using a computer should be competent typists with a good knowledge of word processing.

The introduction of the explanatory note on the certificate is a cause of concern to the Dyslexia Association of Ireland (DAI) and to parents. It is a permanent statement on the certificate of the student. For future employers, who may not be familiar with dyslexia and its effects, the wording of the different explanatory notes might give the impression that the student could not read or write. This is more important for the student who opts for employment directly after second level. There is no such explanatory note on the certificates, diplomas and degrees issued by third-level colleges and PLC courses and employers, in all probability, will not ask to see the Junior or Leaving Certificates of applicants with further qualifications.

In 2006 the Equality Tribunal ruled that the practice of annotating certificates of students who received reasonable accommodation was discriminatory. The Department of Education and Science mounted a legal challenge to this decision and a court ruling in this matter is expected in the autumn of 2007.

Application Procedure

For the Junior Certificate, applications are made in October/November prior to the exam. For Junior Certificate students, the application process is less rigorous than at Leaving Certificate level. The form is simpler and there is no need for an assessment to accompany the application. Accommodations are usually granted if the school applies for them.

Application for special arrangements at Leaving Certificate are made by the School authorities, usually in May of the year before the exam is taken. Schools should include an up to date psycho-educational assessment report and samples of the student's work to the Dept. of Education and Science to support the application. Parents must sign this application. The application is processed through NEPS. The NEPS psychologist comes to the school to interview the student and staff. In some cases additional testing may be carried out. The psychologist decides if the accommodation is granted. If an application is turned down, there is an appeals procedure.

Entry to Third Level

Entry to third level institutions: universities; institutes of technology; nursing and some other colleges, is by application to the Central Applications Office. The CAO form should be completed and returned to the CAO office by February 1st of the year in which the student takes the Leaving Certificate. Ten courses at degree level and ten courses at national certificate or diploma level can be requested. Change of mind forms can be submitted up until the end of the exams usually. (Check the website www.cao.ie for precise dates). The courses should be listed in the order of the student's preference. If the student would love to study veterinary science but is afraid of not attaining the required number of points, he/she should still list it as first choice. Students are offered the highest preference on their list to which their points entitle them. If there are second round offers and a place becomes available on a higher preference course the student will be offered this, even if he/she has already accepted a first round offer.

Note: It is very important to indicate on the CAO form if a student has dyslexia. A Supplementary Information Form (SIF) will be sent to all applicants who indicate that they have a disability such as dyslexia. They may qualify for consideration under the Supplementary Admission system operated by universities and colleges. In order to do so students are required to submit: Evidence of Disability; Psycho-educational Assessment Report; Personal Statement and Second Level Academic References.

Psycho-educational Assessment Reports must be no more than 3 years old. This is very important as older reports will not be considered valid. The report, signed by the assessing psychologist is usually regarded as evidence of disability for students with dyslexia.

The Psycho-educational Assessment Reports must be thorough and specific and carried out by a fully qualified psychologist. It must be clearly stated in the report that dyslexia/specific learning disability has been diagnosed. A note indicating the granting of reasonable accommodations in the Leaving Certificate is not considered sufficient. Age appropriate standardized tests must be used, giving data for overall academic ability and attainments in reading, writing and spelling.

The Personal Statement must be written by the student and must be as detailed as possible. It is important for the student to explain his/her difficulties and why he/she has chosen a particular course, and outline any factors which may help the student to complete the course satisfactorily. For example, the student may have had work experience or summer employment in the area, or pursued a relevant hobby.

The Second Level Academic Reference is provided by the school principal and teacher/guidance counselor completing the relevant form. Details of any learning support provided by the school and strategies used by the student to cope with learning should be included.

For further information consult the CAO website www.cao.ie. The relevant section is called 'Common Supplementary Admission Criteria for the selection of Students with Disabilities and Specific Learning Difficulties'. Information is also available on the DAI site www.dyslexia.ie

Special arrangements at third level

Many third level colleges and examination bodies make provision for dyslexic students taking written exams. These provisions can include being given extra time, being allowed to use a tape recorder or word processor when taking the exam, and having the specific learning difficulty taken into account when marking the exam paper. No annotation appears on the certificates of students who receive special accommodation at third level. Students should consult the Disability Officer, Course Tutor or Director for precise details of what is available.

How Parents can Help Children with Dyslexia

Self-esteem – the foundation of success

One of the most devastating effects of dyslexia, particularly if the condition has not been diagnosed, is the damage it does to self-esteem. It is impossible to over-estimate the pain and frustration of children exposed every day to failure in the classroom situation. Schoolwork requires the child to face reading, writing and spelling every day and if a student experiences difficulties in these areas then each day is a trial. Children are very aware of their own ranking in class, even if this is not commented on by parents or teachers.

Children with dyslexia get tired more easily from schoolwork because they have to work so much harder just to keep up. Sometimes the effort they put into homework will not be reflected in their results and they may need a lot of encouragement to keep trying. Parents will need to keep in constant touch with the child's school, sharing information and assessment reports with class and special needs teachers. A difficult balance has to be maintained between acting as advocate for your child in the school situation and intruding into the domain of the teacher.

In order to preserve self-esteem it is very important that a student is rewarded for effort rather than results. Improvements can be measured against previous performance of the student and not against that of the highest achieving person in the class. Oral contributions to class should be acknowledged and any illustrations or practical work taken into account.

Praise and encouragement are very important but the child must know that it is genuine. Descriptive praise, telling a child what he has done that is valued and why, rather than just saying 'Well done' is the best option. If the first little step that a child makes is not acknowledged and commented on, the next step might not be taken.

Parents can foster self-esteem in students by encouraging any out of school activity in which a child can achieve success. Imagination may have to be exercised to discover such an activity, but it is well worth the effort. Speech and drama, sport, dance, gardening, pet care, computers, swimming, scouting, cooking, chess, painting, fishing, could all yield success for someone with reading difficulties.

Perhaps the most important source of self-esteem is the love and support which parents provide. When children are secure that they are loved for themselves and that approval is not dependent on success at school, they will be less anxious. The great plus for parents is that it costs no money to express your love for your child and it does not require years of training or specialized knowledge. And they can be assured that it will pay dividends in the long run.

Tips For Parents of Pre-Adolescent Children With Specific Learning Difficulties

Helping your child with homework

1. Provide a quiet, warm, well lit, comfortable place for your child to work.
2. Always stay close at hand. Be there when your child needs you.
3. Be aware of and control the amount of time and energy spent on each activity. If you feel too much is spent on any specific subject, discuss it with the teacher. Try to negotiate a compromise so that your child can get all homework done within a reasonable time for his age and class.
4. Check with your child beforehand on what exactly he/she has to do and how it is to be presented. See the teacher if your child experiences specific difficulties, especially in writing down assignments in school. Ask the teacher to write them on the board or talk slower and repeat several times or to actually check that the child has written it down correctly.
5. Make sure your child has all the materials needed (pens, pencils, paper, rulers, markers, etc.)
6. Praise your child. Don't pressurise, criticise or make false promises.
7. Provide usable and readable reference books as needed (dictionaries, encyclopaedias, atlases, etc.).

8. Read and spell (on paper) any word your child requires. Don't try to start a reading or spelling lesson when your child is trying to do homework or he/she won't ask next time. Make separate times for reading and spelling.

Working with your child
1. Set aside specific times during the day to work with your child. Let these times be for you and your child alone.
2. Start with short work periods and gradually increase them. A good rule is to stop when your child is at the peak of success. Don't push him or her to the point of failure.
3. Be as objective and as patient as you can. Speak to your child in a quiet, firm voice.
4. Make commands or directions short and simple.
5. If a task is too difficult for your child, move on to something easier. Then come back to the first task after changing it so that your child can succeed. Never introduce a task by saying or implying it is easy. Never compare to siblings.
6. When your child is capable of doing a task, gently insist that he/she finish it.
7. Be aware of your child's abilities as well as his/her weaknesses. Don't continue using tasks that are too easy for your child. There should be some challenge to hold your child's attention.
8. Praise your child for even the smallest success. Do not emphasise failure.
9. Really listen to your child. He/she can often tell you the best ways to help.
10. Relax with your child. Both of you should enjoy your time together.

Never underestimate the power of informal learning and fun activities. So many games teach important social skills such as sharing, rules, taking turns, winning and losing. Playing board games can also develop the key skills needed for literacy. Problem solving, strategic thinking, mathematical skills, balance and fine motor coordination can all be learned through games. These activities can take the 'work' out of working with your child.

Listening to your child read

Set aside a 10-15 minute period each day when you can read with your child. Choose a place free of distractions, like other children or the TV. Then follow the steps for paired reading set out below.

1. Ask your child to choose a book to read.
2. Sit side by side, so both of you can see the text.
3. Begin by reading the text together. Adjust your speed and rhythm so you are both reading in time together.
4. When your child is ready to read alone, he or she should tap you on the arm. This is the signal for you to be silent and let your child read alone.
5. When your child gets a word wrong or can't read a word, don't let him or her struggle for more than 5 seconds. Just tell your child what the word is. Let them read it correctly and praise them for it. Don't analyse the word phonically and try to teach them how to spell it. Just tell them. Then praise them when they say it right.
6. Don't read for more than 15 minutes. Talk with your child about the story you have read. Ask questions posed by the story. Answer any questions your child may have.

Children who do paired reading with their parents show reading improvements at 3 times the speed of children who don't do paired reading. This conclusion was drawn by Dr. Keith Topping, Dundee University, from research on hundreds of children with reading problems. Paired reading allows children to read interesting material, to control the amount of help they get from you, to be praised for success and to get as little criticism as possible. Above all paired reading allows a dyslexic child to experience fluent reading. This experience of fluent reading will motivate your child to put in the homework necessary to learn how to read fluently.

Helping your child learn spellings
Set aside a 10 minute period each day for helping your child with spelling. Spelling lists should be short; no more than five words. The same spelling list should be worked on for 3 nights in a row. This means that no more than 10 new words can be learned in a week. Follow the routine described for each word.

1. Write the target word out or make it with plastic letters.
2. Tell your child how to say the word and what it means if he or she doesn't know.
3. Ask your child to copy the target word and to say the name of each letter as it is being written.
4. Ask your child to look at what they have written and to say the whole word.
5. Ask your child to check that what they have written is the same as the target word. This checking is done letter by letter from the target to the copy.

6. Your child should then try to write and say the target word from memory. If he or she makes any mistakes, cross the word out and start again.
7. Repeat step 6 until the word has been written correctly 3 times.
8. Make sure your child practises each word following this routine for 3 consecutive daily sessions.

This way of learning spelling is called the SOS method – Simultaneous Oral Spelling. Dr. Lynette Bradley at Oxford University has shown that this method is almost twice as effective as simple writing or repetition. SOS is a multi-sensory learning method. When your child uses the SOS method, he/she is using all sensory channels to learn how to spell new words. He/she is using visual, auditory and motor/movement channels to take in the spelling pattern of the new target word. Your child is also using his/her intelligence to check that they have not jumbled the order of letters by mistake. The SOS method also involves over learning. Each word is practised for 3 days in a row. This helps your child remember each new word he/she learns. The method is slow. Only 10 new words can be learned per week. However, it is effective.

Maths and Dyscalculia

Many people are surprised to find that more than half of children with dyslexia also have difficulty with mathematics, particularly arithmetic. However, this is not surprising when one thinks of the processes involved in dealing with maths and the core difficulties which affect children with dyslexia. In order to cope with, say, arithmetic problems, the child needs competence in the following areas:

Language – to understand the words used in stating the problem. This is important because of the many different ways of describing the same operation in arithmetic, eg. 'subtract', 'take away', 'less', 'minus', etc.

Reading – to understand what is being asked. Questions are often phrased in an indirect and confusing manner.

Short-term (working) memory – to remember the various pieces of information given in the question, eg. if Mary has 5 apples and Tom has 3 apples more than Mary and Betty has twice as many as Tom, how many does Betty have? Poor working memory is a particular problem when dealing with mental arithmetic.

Number manipulation – in order to add, subtract, multiply or divide

Sequential memory – to remember number facts such as times tables, or the steps required in solving a problem

Orientation – to know where to begin when adding or subtracting and later where to place decimal points

Interpreting abstract symbols – to understand mathematical symbols and distinguish between the similar ones. Children who confuse b and d, or p and q are likely to have difficulties with the plus and multiplication symbols, and the subtraction and division ones.

Thus, many of the difficulties which affect children when learning to read and spell also cause problems with mathematics. For some students the difficulties may be caused by their levels of reading, language and memory, while for others the difficulty may be a more fundamental problem in grasping the underlying concepts and in performing calculations. In the latter case, the problem may be diagnosed as dyscalculia and one to one support may be necessary.

How parents can help

Be positive about mathematics – do not pass on any negative feelings which might give the child the idea that maths is a difficult subject. Mahesh Sharma, an expert on the study of mathematics, has with tongue in cheek identified a disease called 'mathephobia' which he says is very widespread. He alleges that children catch it from their parents.

Many children suffer from what is called 'maths anxiety'. This is a reaction of fear and distress when faced with mathematical problems. This may well be because so much stress is laid on quick responses in maths. It seems that it is not enough to be able to work out a problem, but one must be able to work it out quickly. This may apply particularly when mental arithmetic problems or time tables are being dealt with in class. In the same way as teachers may be requested not to ask the child with dyslexia to read aloud in class without prior warning, it might be possible to ask that the child not be asked rapid fire questions in mathematics, and that the child be allowed to use a number square or table book if remembering tables is a problem.

When asked to assist with maths homework parents may inadvertently end up confusing the child by using a different problem solving method than that used in school. It might be wise to consult the class teacher about how best to help in a given situation and where a child has enduring difficulties with maths it may be best to get professional help.

Younger children can be greatly helped in developing an understanding of number concepts through daily activities. Practical and concrete experience of number and computation can be given when shopping (how many bread rolls/bananas/eggs etc. are needed). Setting a table can be used to demonstrate orientation – left and right – and again numbers of plates, glasses, knives, forks, spoons required. Simple board games involving numbers and dice such as Snakes and Ladders are great learning tools. Cooking and baking which involve weighing and counting ingredients, and cross checking with recipes for time of cooking and temperature of oven are very enjoyable ways of using numbers.

There are some good computer programmes available (see Computers and Assistive Technology below) which can help children develop skills in a fun way. Parents may discover more information by reading any of the following:

Chinn, S. 'Dealing with Dyscalculia', London, Souvenir Press, 2007.

Henderson, A. 'Maths for the Dyslexic: A Practical Guide', London, David Fulton, 2000.

Kay, J. and Yeo, D. 'Dyslexia and Maths', London, David Fulton, 2003.

Computers and Assistive Technology

Developments in computers and assistive technology have been of great benefit to all students, and in particular provide essential and significant help to students with dyslexia. Computer programmes can be used to assist the learning process. While there is no substitute for individual tuition from a trained teacher, computer programmes provide valuable reinforcement and variety and can increase motivation. There are hundreds of programmes available which can be used to practice reading, word attack skills, spelling and maths; there are also many assistive programmes which enable learners to access material, while others support writing and learning.

Access to even a basic word processor with spell check can be helpful for many people with dyslexia. It removes the anxiety of writing with pen and paper, and it is much easier to make changes or reorganize the sequence of the written work. A spell check facility is also very helpful; it is easier and quicker than checking a dictionary and can be done independently rather than having to ask for help with a spelling. Good keyboard skills are essential, so it is important to learn proper touch-typing. Scanners, which allow text to be put directly onto a computer, and screen reading software which reads this material aloud, are extremely helpful to people who find reading tiring or difficult. Voice operated software allows the user to dictate directly onto the computer without having to worry about spelling which makes producing written work much easier and speedier.

With so many programmes and products available, it is easy to become confused with the choice. Computer software can be expensive and comes packaged, so it can be difficult to find out prior to purchase if a product is suitable. Ways of obtaining practical experience of the software include advice from teachers, demonstrations of software at conferences or exhibitions; it can sometimes be possible to get free 30-day demo or trial disks from suppliers or download them from the internet. Ideally the teacher, parent and most importantly the intended user should be involved in the process.

Currently, for primary or second level students with significant dyslexia, whose literacy skills are at the 2nd percentile or lower, the school can apply to the SENO for a computer/laptop and any specialist software needed by the individual student. If parents buy a computer and/or software for a child with dyslexia for home/personal use, the VAT can be claimed back, using Form VAT 61A, from the VAT Repayments Section, Revenue Commissioners, The Plantation, Monaghan. Tel. 047 81425. Forms can be downloaded from the website www.revenue.ie

Some Simple Low-cost Technology
It can be very helpful if teachers provide students with typed or word processed notes rather than handwritten ones.

Photocopying information or printing onto coloured paper. Some people find that they get less glare or experience less visual stress when using colours. Some students use coloured overlays, which they place over the textbook. It is also possible to change the font colour and background colour on the computer.

Colour coding key information can aid memory; using different coloured highlighters, or colour coding in documents, should be encouraged.

Some material is available on tape/CD, particularly English novels, drama and even some poetry. This can be accessed through most good bookshops, libraries or online. DVDs may also be available where novels or dramas have been filmed. These would all be good interactive learning tools.

Third level students who learn best by hearing, benefit from taping/recording lectures, even recording their own study notes. They can build up their own audio library which they can then use for revision. An MP3 player can be used so that the student can listen to their class or study notes while travelling on the bus. Some students may even end up doing their exams on tape.

An electronic dictionary is an in-expensive, portable tool for checking spelling, e.g. Franklin Spellmaster. As long as the individual can make a reasonable phonetic attempt, there is a good chance that the correct spelling can be identified. Some electronic dictionaries also have a thesaurus feature which can help with expanding vocabulary.

Developing Keyboard Skills

Computer literacy is a skill for life, and to be able to use a word processor effectively all students should learn to touch type properly. It does take time and effort but it is well worth it, and best to start early, before any bad habits develop. Regular practice is the key, and there is a wide range of typing tutor programmes available for all ages, eg. Type to Learn, Englishtype Junior and Senior, and Mavis Beacon.

If the use of a word processor helps students to achieve, they should be able to produce homework, projects and house exams in this way.

The reasonable accommodations allowed in state and college examinations include the use of a word processor for some students, though this facility is less common at second than at third level. If the school is to assess whether a student would benefit from using a word processor in examinations, the student needs to be proficient in its use. This means, in the case of a Junior Certificate student, that good keyboarding skills should be in place by the end of second year.

Developing reading, spelling and numeracy skills
There are hundreds of excellent programmes available which support the development of basic skills in reading, phonics, spelling, and maths. However, it must be remembered that no computer programme is a substitute for individualised specialist teaching. Many programmes will also come in a range of different levels; it is important to choose the right level for each individual. Catalogues of educational software can be obtained from many of the specialist suppliers listed at the end of this section. The programmes mentioned below are examples of the types commonly used.

There are many literacy programmes available which provide a useful learning aid to practise and develop reading, phonics, spelling, etc. Especially for younger readers, there is a wide selection of talking books available, eg. the Wellington Square and Oxford Reading Tree schemes.

Wordshark, based on the 'Alpha to Omega' programme, combines the excitement of computer games with learning to spell and read. It offers 41 games that use sound, graphics and text to teach and reinforce word recognition and spelling. New words and vocabularies can also be added.

The Lexia reading series helps students to strengthen skills through interactive exercises working on areas such as phonemic awareness, decoding skills and comprehension.

Starspell helps develop spelling skills from younger children to adults. It uses the Look-Cover-Write-Check strategy. Every word is spoken and many have pictures. It is also possible to create personal word lists and subject specific vocabularies.

The Gamz Player CD is based on the popular swap card games, and contains many additional features to support reading, phonics and spelling.

Nessy is designed to reinforce spelling, reading and listening skills in a multi-sensory way. It includes printable card games, activity sheets, mnemonics and computer games with good graphics.

There are many other programmes which target specific areas, such as reading comprehension and cloze procedures, auditory discrimination and phonics, the magic 'e' rule, etc. These can be useful motivational tools to reinforce learning.

Some children with dyslexia have problems with numeracy. Maths software programmes provide opportunity to practise arithmetic skills and reinforce maths concepts. Numbershark, Mathmania, the BBC Maths Workshop Series, IntelliMathics and the Maths Circus Series are all useful programmes. Learning how to use a calculator and also simple spreadsheets can also aid the performance of calculations.

Reading support/accessing text

For students with reading difficulties, accessing curriculum textbooks can be very difficult and time consuming. For those students whose reading is reasonably competent, but where they come across occasional words that they cannot identify, a reading pen is a good solution, eg. Quicktionary Reading Pen. These are hand held pens containing OCR software which enables them to scan and read words and phrases; they also include a dictionary to explain what a word means.

Students who have more significant reading difficulty may need to go for a complete text-to-speech option, using screen reading software. Screen reading software will read any text on the computer screen, whether it is text which the student has just typed, an email or webpage, or pages of a textbook which have been scanned into the computer. When used together a scanner and screen reading package can make even very slow readers self-sufficient. The reading voice and reading speed can be adjusted; words can be read word-by-word, in sentences or continuous passages. Text scanned in can be converted to an audio file format and downloaded onto an MP3 player to be listened to later.

Examples of this type of screen reading programme are ClaroRead, Kurzweil and TextHelp. ClaroRead and TextHELP have additional features supporting the production of written work, eg. talking spell checker, homophone checkers and predictive typing. ClaroRead works closely alongside Dragon Dictate (see below) resulting in seamless dictation and proof reading of text. Mobile versions of this type of software are now becoming available (the programme comes on a USB drive); this means that the student can carry the software with them and use it on any compatible computer.

Writing support

Access to even a basic word processing programme can be helpful, and a student with dyslexia will produce better work on a computer than if they were handwriting. The computer will always produce clear legible writing, whereas handwriting may be difficult to read. Spelling can be checked using the spellchecker. Editing and rearranging text is easy, so students do not have to rewrite laboriously to produce a final draft. This facility also helps students who have sequencing difficulties as it is easy to edit the text so as to rearrange the sequence. Forgotten information can simply be added in later, or a paragraph moved to improve the flow of the passage.

Screen readers are also a very useful tool for supporting writing. They allow the student to hear any errors, eg. a mis-typed word, or an incomplete sentence. ClaroRead and TextHELP also have a homophone checker; possible homonyms are identified in the text and the student is then given guidance to help identify whether they have the correct word. Both programmes also have word prediction.

Software such as Textease, Co:Writer and Penfriend support writing with features such as talking spellcheckers, which makes the choosing of the correct spelling easier, and word prediction, which can increase the speed of written production and in so doing increase the student's confidence in their writing ability. Clicker is another useful programme where you can write with whole words and even pictures.

Voice recognition software, which was originally designed so that astronauts could use computers while tucked up in their space suits, is ideally suited for older students and adults who have to produce extended pieces of written work such as long essays. All instructions can be given verbally; the computer will type as you speak. Dragon Dictate Naturally Speaking is the most commonly used programme of this type. While this type of software has improved greatly over the last decade, it will rarely be 100% accurate. There is an initial training period where the programme learns about the user's voice, and the accuracy does improve with usage, as each time the programme is used it learns more about the user's voice, speech patterns and the vocabulary commonly used. A compatible digital voice recorder can be used with Dragon; this means that documents can be created by voice anywhere, and when the digital recorder is synched with the PC, Dragon can then transcribe the document.

To get the best from both screen reading and voice recognition software a powerful, modern computer, with a good soundcard is essential; these programmes either may not work at all or else work poorly on older machines. A good quality microphone is also important, ideally one that limits external noise which can distract or confuse the software.

Organisational & Study Skills

A very common feature of dyslexia is poor organisation skills, which affects many areas, eg. time-keeping, planning study timetables, and especially the organisation of information, whether it is making good revision notes or the organisation of longer written passages.

Mind-mapping software programmes are very useful tools for students who have good visual-spatial ability. Information can be converted into a visual mind-map containing key information, pictures and showing connections. Students can use mind-mapping software to create visual revision aids, but it can also be used for brainstorming, concept mapping and planning essays. Kidspiration (for younger students) and Inspiration are some of the most commonly used programmes of this type.

Wordswork is a multi-sensory programme on study skills. While it was designed primarily for undergraduate students with dyslexia, it is relevant for students at second level, and also for adults, particularly those who want to improve their skills before going back to formal education. It uses graphics, voice-overs, colour and humour to develop a variety of skills which students with dyslexia (and others) need to address. Topics covered include essay writing, memory strategies, exam revision and time management. It also includes sections on reading, spelling, grammar and other areas.

There are some programmes on the market which may help to improve memory using various interactive activities and games, eg. Mastering Memory. They present sequences of pictures, words and symbols to be remembered, and gradually increase the difficulty level and speed.

Some older students and adults find using a PDA (Personal Digital Assistant) or electronic organiser helpful to keep track of coursework requirements, when an essay or project is due, making to-do lists and study timetables.

Useful Websites with Information on the Use of Technology in Education:

National Centre for Technology in Education (NCTE)
www.ncte.ie

British Educational Communications
and Technology Agency (BECTA)
www.becta.org.uk

British Dyslexia Association (BDA)
www.bdadyslexia.org.uk

iAnsyst Ltd
www.dyslexic.com

Specialist Suppliers
A wide variety of software and hardware catalogues are available from the suppliers listed below.

Award Systems
38 Pine Valley Park, Grange Road, Dublin 16.
Tel: 01 4930011 Website: www.awardsys.net

Carroll Education Ltd
34A Lavery Avenue Park West, Dublin 12.
Tel: 01 6120860 Website: www.carrolleducation.ie

Diskovery
Unit 2, Waveney, Howth Harbour, Co. Dublin.
Tel: 01 8063910 Website: www.diskovery.ie

Easy PC
Unit M7, Smithtown Ind Estate, Shannon, Co. Clare.
Tel. 061 719537 Website: www.easypc.ie

Edtech Software Ltd
Murrisk, Westport, Co. Mayo.
Tel: 098 64886 Website: www.edtech.ie

GAMZ
25 Albert Park Rd, Malvern, Worcestershire
WR14 1HW, England.
Tel: 0044 1684 562158 Website: www.gamzuk.com

iAnsyst Ltd
Fen House, Fen Road, Chesterton, Cambridge
CB4 1UN, England.
Tel. 0044 1223 420101 Website: www.iansyst.co.uk
and www.dyslexic.com

Jackson Technology
24 Kiltipper Avenue, Aylesbury, Dublin 24.
Tel: 01 4518508 and 01 4624793
Website: www.jacksontechnology.com
and www.dyslexia-ireland.com

Scanning Pens Ltd
6 The Quadrant, Newark Close, Royston
SC85HL, England.
Tel: 0044 87 07203310
Website: www.scanningpens.co.uk

TextHelp Systems Ltd
Enkalon Business Centre, 25 Randalstown Road,
Antrim, B41 4LJ Northern Ireland.
Tel: 048 84942810 Website: www.texthelp.com

Major Special Needs Software Publishers

Most of their software can be bought from the suppliers listed above.

Crick Software	www.cricksoft.com
Don Johnston	www.donjohnston.com
Inclusive Technology Ltd	www.inclusive.co.uk
Inspiration Software	www.inspiration.com
Riverdeep Learning	www.riverdeep-learning.co.uk
Semerc	www.semerc.com
Sherston	www.sherston.com

Alternative Therapies

The Dyslexia Association has been working with children and adults with SLD/Dyslexia since 1972. The association advocates direct teaching as the optimum way of improving literacy skills. Teaching is time-consuming and often tedious, but when appropriate teaching, as an intervention, begins early in life and has the moral and practical support of the home and the school, it is successful. All teaching is most effective when it adheres to the following basic principles:

1. The results of the assessment are used to diagnose specific learning difference.
2. Learning objectives are used for planning and evaluation.
3. The teaching is multi-sensory, using all available learning channels.
4. The teaching is systematic/sequential, ie. uses task analysis.
5. The teaching is cumulative, ie. helps the learner connect what is being learned to what is already known.
6. The teaching provides for over-learning, ie. repetition and consolidation, through rehearsal to automaticity.
7. The teaching is cognitive and encourages learners to think about language and understand language structures.
8. The teaching is success orientated, ie. it ensures success and builds self esteem.
9. The learner is helped to transfer learning to real literacy situations.
10. The home is involved.

The Dyslexia Association's years of experience and knowledge of SLD/Dyslexia, as well as our contact with British, European and International associations, has led us to the conclusion that there is no quick fix, no magic pill, no universal panacea, that will provide a cure.

Despite this belief, regularly, over the years, bona fide researchers and charlatans alike continue to look for alternative treatments that might cure, prevent or otherwise have a positive effect on the learning difficulty. Learning difficulties and dyslexia in particular, seem to attract unusual forms of treatment. The only real way to determine the worth of these treatments is to become better acquainted with some of the methods of scientific investigation. Research has shown that many things can influence performance incidentally:

- Placebo Effects – in placebo effects, illnesses can be 'cured' just because patients believe that they are receiving effective treatment.
- Hawthorne effects – the Hawthorne effect is the finding that for every change in circumstances there will be a change in behaviour.
- Attentional effects – in attentional effects, subjects may react favourably to a treatment just because they are the centre of a lot of attention.
- Motivational effects – motivational effects are the result of a subject trying much harder just because they have been singled out for treatment and made to feel special.

Parents and professionals should watch out for any promoted method or product that costs a lot of money and promises a quick fix or 'cure'. Any method or product should be considered controversial and suspect if:

1. There is no research to prove that it works, or which explains why it works.
2. The research has not been independently replicated.
3. The claims of the method or product far exceed the research results.
4. The only 'proof' is the personal testimony of parents or their children.

Before signing any contract, agreeing to any treatment or purchasing any product that sounds too good to be true, ask to see the independent research papers that support their claims. Also ask for local references. Talk to professionals in the field about the method. If it sounds too good to be true, it probably is.

Non-teaching Interventions

A range of non-teaching interventions has been developed in recent years. Most of these interventions claim that, by providing additional stimulus and a systematic programme that develops an aspect of the child's functioning, their therapy also results in improved literacy skills. Reading is not something which develops naturally, it is a skill which has to be taught and so while non-teaching interventions can help some children who have deficits in particular areas of processing, they will continue to need informed teaching.

Interventions can be roughly categorized under a number of headings viz.

- Exercise and Movement
- Auditory Stimulaton
- Visual correction
- Diet

Exercise and Movement

These therapies include educational kinesiology, neuro-developmental therapy, primary movement, brain gym, DDAT programme. The main therapies are based on theories of development and how various movements that the child should make have failed to develop appropriately. The therapies attempt, by a programme of movement, to remediate these developmental delays or bad habits. They include such programmes as neurodevelopmental therapy, Primary Movement, Brain Gym.

One movement therapy, DDAT, is based on what is known as the cerebellar theory of dyslexia. This proposes that the cerebellum, which is the part of the brain that, among other functions, controls balance and movement can be retrained. There has been considerable controversy in recent times over the research methodology related to this programme cf. Dyslexia, May 2003.

Auditory Stimulation

These include sound therapies and the Mozart Effect, ie. the belief that the rhythms and cadences of Mozart's music improve brain activity.

Visual Correction

A number of therapies concentrate on the visual aspects of dyslexia. They note that some persons with dyslexia experience difficulty with eye control, eye-tracking, convergence, while others report difficulty with 'blurring' print, sensitivity to black print on white background. This has led to the development of colour testing, prescribing coloured lenses and overlays and a range of visual-based remedial programmes. There remains some controversy over Scotopic sensitivity, more often now called Meares-Irlen Syndrome or visual stress, but anecdotal evidence suggests that the use of lenses and overlays do remove some of the discomfort of reading. However, the difficulties may be independent of dyslexia and the child will still need to be taught the structure of the written language.

Nutritional Supplements/Diet

There is a body of influential research which has been examining the effects of certain EFAs (essential fatty acids) and HUFAs (Highly Unsaturated Fatty Acids) on brain function. These essential fatty acids are found in oily fish (eg. salmon, tuna, and mackerel) and in vegetable oils and seeds (eg. sunflower, flax, pumpkin and sesame).

Useful Resources

Books

Ball, M, Hughes, A and McCormack, W.
'Dyslexia – an Irish Perspective',
Blackhall Publishing, 2006.

Culligan, B.
'Improving Children's Spelling,
A Guide for Teachers and Parents',
Dublin, Elo Press, 1997.

McCormack, W.
'Lost for Words: Dyslexia at Second Level and Beyond.
A Practical Guide for Parents and Teachers',
Tower Press, 2007.

Ott, P.
'How to Detect and Manage Dyslexia',
Heinemann, 1997.

Reid, G.
'Dyslexia – A Complete Guide for Parents',
John Wiley & Sons, 2004.

Government Publications

Report of the Task Force on Dyslexia,
Government of Ireland, 2002

Understanding Dyslexia,
Video, CD ROM and DVD, 2005

(This is a most useful resource, one which has been
distributed by the Department of Education and Science
to all schools. Parents should ask for a showing of the
video or DVD at a parents' or staff meeting).

Websites

Organisations

www.ahead.ie	Association for Higher Education Access and Disability
www.bda-dyslexia.org.uk	British Dyslexia Association
www.cao.ie	Central Applications Office with links to the Higher Education Institutions websites
www.dyslexia.ie	Dyslexia Association of Ireland
www.education.ie	Department of Education & Science
www.ncte.ie	National Council for Technology in Education
www.scoilnet.ie	Site for primary and post-primary schools
www.psihq.ie	Psychological Society of Ireland
www.sess.ie	Special Education Support Service

Study Skills Websites

www.skoool.ie	Subject notes and lots more
www.learnforsuccess.info	Study skills

Educational suppliers for learning materials:
STA, Surgisales Teaching Aids
252 Harold's Cross Road, Dublin 6W;
branch also in Kilkenny.
Tel: 01-4966688

Formative Fun
Branches currently in Dublin, Dundalk, Galway,
Kilkenny, Letterkenny, Limerick and Wexford.

The Early Learning Centre
Branches currently in Dublin, Galway, Limerick
and Waterford.

Hornsby International Dyslexia Centre
Wye Street, London SW11 2HB, England.
Tel: 0044-20-72231144
Website: www.hornsby.co.uk
Email: dyslexia@hornsby.co.uk

Helen Arkell Dyslexia Centre
Frensham, Farnham, Surrey GU10 3BW, England.

DAI Membership

DAI is a voluntary organisation and a registered charity. We rely greatly on the support we get from members to pay our bills.

Membership of DAI costs €40 a year (from 1.1.2008) and is open to all. Only one membership is needed per family. Members receive a card each year which must be produced when enrolling a child at a DAI Workshop, Summer School or with a DAI listed tutor. Only members of the association may avail of these DAI services.

Membership fees go to cover the costs of running the national association. The national association is a resource for all of the country. It provides:

- An information/support service available through our national office to members, parents, teachers and members of the public.
- Information/support to existing branches and to new groups, as well as access to our group insurance scheme.
- Newsletters, issued at least three times a year.
- Lobbying and negotiation with the Department of Education and Science which have been carried on for over 25 years. These have resulted in greatly increased awareness and many advances in facilities for students with dyslexia. The effect of this can only be judged by looking back.
- DAI also acts as a service provider offering assessment, specialist tuition, and training.
- Grants from fundraising initiatives, eg. the Hasbro NGPW fund.

Your membership fee helps to ensure that the association will be there whenever you need it.